AN EXCITING TALE AND AN ANIMAL'S TAIL

TRICKY, STICKY WORDS

By STEPHEN O'CONOR

Illustrations by ANNABEL TEMPEST

Music by DREW TEMPERANTE

CANTATA
LEARNING

WWW.CANTATALEARNING.COM

CANTATA
LEARNING

Published by Cantata Learning
1710 Roe Crest Drive
North Mankato, MN 56003
www.cantatalearning.com

Copyright © 2018 Cantata Learning

All rights reserved. No part of this publication may be reproduced
in any form without written permission from the publisher.

A note to educators and librarians from the publisher: Cantata Learning has provided the following data to assist in book processing and suggested use of Cantata Learning product.

Publisher's Cataloging-in-Publication Data
Prepared by Librarian Consultant: Ann-Marie Begnaud
Library of Congress Control Number: 2016938094
    An Exciting Tale and an Animal's Tail : Tricky, Sticky Words
    Series: Read, Sing, Learn
    By Stephen O'Conor
    Illustrations by Annabel Tempest
    Music by Drew Temperante
    Summary: Learn about homophones, words that sound alike but are spelled differently and have different meanings, in this playful song.
    ISBN: 978-1-63290-798-1 (library binding/CD)
Suggested Dewey and Subject Headings:
    Dewey: E 428.1
    LCSH Subject Headings: Homonyms – Juvenile literature. | Homonyms – Songs and music – Texts. | Homonyms – Juvenile sound recordings.
    Sears Subject Headings: English language – Homonyms. | School songbooks. | Children's songs. | Popular music.
    BISAC Subject Headings: JUVENILE NONFICTION / Language Arts / Vocabulary & Spelling. | JUVENILE NONFICTION / Music / Songbooks.

Book design and art direction: Tim Palin Creative
Editorial direction: Flat Sole Studio
Music direction: Elizabeth Draper
Music written and produced by Drew Temperante

Printed in the United States of America in North Mankato, Minnesota.
072017   0367CGF17

ACCESS THE MUSIC!

SCAN CODE WITH MOBILE APP

CANTATALEARNING.COM

TIPS TO SUPPORT LITERACY AT HOME

WHY READING AND SINGING WITH YOUR CHILD IS SO IMPORTANT

Daily reading with your child leads to increased academic achievement. Music and songs, specifically rhyming songs, are a fun and easy way to build early literacy and language development. Music skills correlate significantly with both phonological awareness and reading development. Singing helps build vocabulary and speech development. And reading and appreciating music together is a wonderful way to strengthen your relationship.

READ AND SING EVERY DAY!

TIPS FOR USING CANTATA LEARNING BOOKS AND SONGS DURING YOUR DAILY STORY TIME

1. As you sing and read, point out the different words on the page that rhyme. Suggest other words that rhyme.

2. Memorize simple rhymes such as Itsy Bitsy Spider and sing them together. This encourages comprehension skills and early literacy skills.

3. Use the questions in the back of each book to guide your singing and storytelling.

4. Read the included sheet music with your child while you listen to the song. How do the music notes correlate to the words of the song?

5. Sing along on the go and at home. Access music by scanning the QR code on each Cantata book. You can also stream or download the music for free to your computer, smartphone, or mobile device.

Devoting time to daily reading shows that you are available for your child. Together, you are building language, literacy, and listening skills.

Have fun reading and singing!

Come here and hear a song! *Here* and *hear* may sound the same, but they mean two different things. These words are homophones. They sound alike but are not spelled the same and have different meanings.

Are there other tricky, sticky words? Find out by turning the page. Remember to sing along!

Words can be tricky.
Words can be sticky.

We learn about words,
how to say and spell them.

Words can be tricky.
Words can be sticky.

Be sure you know
your way around them.

What will I *wear* to school?
I look through my clothes.

Now *where* is my school?
The bus driver knows.

You put on what you *wear*.
You move to *where* you are going.

Tricky, sticky words
are lots of fun to know!

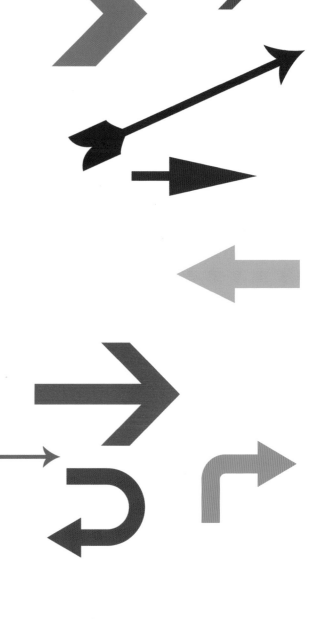

Words can be tricky.
Words can be sticky.

We learn about words,
how to say and spell them.

Words can be tricky.
Words can be sticky.

Be sure you know
your way around them.

Sometimes we *write* at school
with a pencil or a pen.

I hope my spelling's *right*,
or I'll have to try again.

When you *write*, you put down words.
But when you're *right*, hooray for you!

Tricky, sticky words,
you should always learn a few!

Words can be tricky.
Words can be sticky.

We learn about words,
how to say and spell them.

SPELLING Bee

Words can be tricky.
Words can be sticky.

Be sure you know
your way around them.

SPELLING BEE

You want a tight *knot*
when you're tying up your shoes

because it's *not* fun at all
if the *knot* you tied comes loose.

Whoa! Whoa! Whoa! Whoa!
Ahhh! Oh, no. Oops!

Tricky, sticky words
can teach you a thing or two!

Words can be tricky.
Words can be sticky.

We learn about words,
how to say and spell them.

Words can be tricky.

Words can be sticky.

Be sure you know
your way around them.

At school we hear a *tale*
about a princess and a knight.

The knight's horse has a *tail*
sticking through its armor bright.

We all listen to an exciting *tale*.
An animal's *tail* is at the rear.

Tricky, sticky words,
be careful what you hear.
Be careful what you hear!

SONG LYRICS
An Exciting Tale and an Animal's Tail

Words can be tricky.
Words can be sticky.
We learn about words,
how to say and spell them.

Words can be tricky.
Words can be sticky.
Be sure you know
your way around them.

What will I wear to school?
I look through my clothes.
Now where is my school?
The bus driver knows.

You put on what you wear.
You move to where you are going.
Tricky, sticky words
are lots of fun to know!

Words can be tricky.
Words can be sticky.
We learn about words,
how to say and spell them.

Words can be tricky.
Words can be sticky.
Be sure you know
your way around them.

Sometimes we write at school
with a pencil or a pen.
I hope my spelling's right,
or I'll have to try again.

When you write, you put
    down words.
But when you're right, hooray
    for you!
Tricky, sticky words,
you should always learn a few!

Words can be tricky.
Words can be sticky.
We learn about words,
how to say and spell them.

Words can be tricky.
Words can be sticky.
Be sure you know
your way around them.

You want a tight knot
when you're tying up your shoes
because it's not fun at all
if the knot you tied comes loose.

Whoa! Whoa! Whoa! Whoa!
Ahhh! Oh, no. Oops!
Tricky, sticky words
can teach you a thing or two!

Words can be tricky.
Words can be sticky.
We learn about words,
how to say and spell them.

Words can be tricky.
Words can be sticky.
Be sure you know
your way around them.

At school we hear a tale
about a princess and a knight.
The knight's horse has a tail
sticking through its armor bright.

We all listen to an exciting tale.
An animal's tail is at the rear.
Tricky, sticky words,
be careful what you hear.
Be careful what you hear!

An Exciting Tale and an Animal's Tail

Hip Hop
Drew Temperante

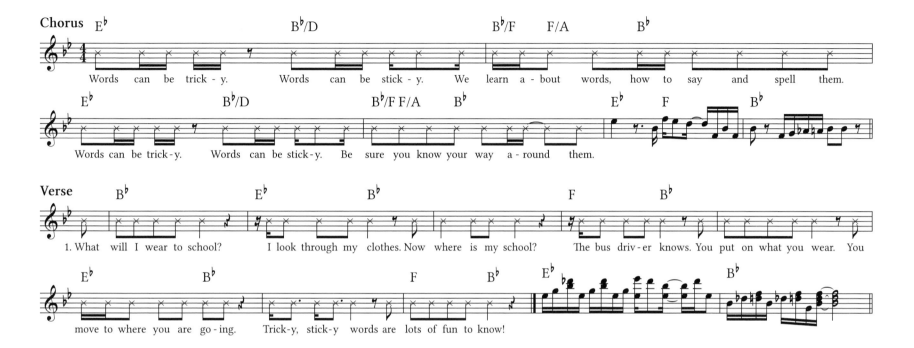

Chorus

Words can be trick-y. Words can be stick-y. We learn a-bout words, how to say and spell them.

Words can be trick-y. Words can be stick-y. Be sure you know your way a-round them.

Verse

1. What will I wear to school? I look through my clothes. Now where is my school? The bus driv-er knows. You put on what you wear. You

move to where you are go-ing. Trick-y, stick-y words are lots of fun to know!

Chorus

Verse 2
Sometimes we write at school
with a pencil or a pen.
I hope my spelling's right,
or I'll have to try again.

When you write, you put down words.
But when you're right, hooray for you!
Tricky, sticky words,
you should always learn a few!

Chorus

Verse 3
You want a tight knot
when you're tying up your shoes
because it's not fun at all
if the knot you tied comes loose.

Whoa! Whoa! Whoa! Whoa!
Ahhh! Oh, no. Oops!
Tricky, sticky words
can teach you a thing or two!

Chorus

Verse 4
At school we hear a tale
about a princess and a knight.
The knight's horse has a tail
sticking through its armor bright.

We all listen to an exciting tale.
An animal's tail is at the rear.
Tricky, sticky words,
be careful what you hear.
Be careful what you hear!

ACCESS THE MUSIC!
SCAN CODE WITH MOBILE APP
CANTATALEARNING.COM

GLOSSARY

Homophones

knot—a tie or snarl in a rope or string

not—a word that means "the opposite of"

tale—a story

tail—a body part that hangs from an animal's rear

write—to put down words on paper or a screen

right—correct

wear—to put on one's body

where—a word that tells about a place's location

GUIDED READING ACTIVITIES

1. Homophones sound the same but have two different meanings. They are also spelled differently. Think of homophones for these words: *eight*, *here*, and *wait*.

2. Write down all the homophones you can think of. Start with those that you learned in this song.

3. Listen to the song again. Every time you hear the word *tricky*, snap your fingers. Every time you hear the word *sticky*, smack your lips. Invent your own moves for other words in the song.

TO LEARN MORE

Cleary, Brian P. *They're There on Their Vacation*. Minneapolis: Millbrook Press, 2015.

Guillain, Charlotte. *Medieval Knights*. North Mankato, MN: Heinemann-Raintree, 2011.

Hall, Michael. *Cat Tale*. New York: Greenwillow Books, 2012.

Jocelyn, Marthe, and Nell Jocelyn. *Where Do You Look?* Toronto: Tundra Books, 2013.